SETTLE UP DARK!

The Holy Spirit's guided light

Written by
Shelvis R. Green III

Illustrated by
Shelvis R. Green III

I would like to dedicate my very first book to my mom and dad, Giselle and Shelvis. They are two loving parents who pay very close attention to all of my life stories. They encourage me to talk about my day EVERYDAY.… I guess it excited them so much that they thought someone would read it. Spoiler alert, there's more books coming. Lolol

Tré wasn't scared of most things.
Some kids found spiders scary... but Tré thought they were pretty cute.
Other kids thought that thunder and lightning were scary... but Tré thought they were exciting and dramatic.
And there were those kids who thought roller coasters were scary... but Tre thought they were nothing less than totally awesome.

But, just like so many people...
... in spite of all the apparently 'scary' things that Tré wasn't scared of at all...
... there was one thing that terrified him from the top of his head down to the tips of his toes...
... the dark

Every time bedtime came around, Tré would talk to himself.
'Tonight's going to be the night,' he'd say.
'Tonight, I'm going to sleep all night.
Tonight, I'm going to stay in my bed.
Tonight, I'm not going to be afraid.'

But it never worked.
A coat on the back of the door would become a gorilla, with huge smashing fists!
A pair of shoes by the bed would become spindly fingers reaching up from the underworld!
A shadow of a tree outside would become a witch hovering outside the window!

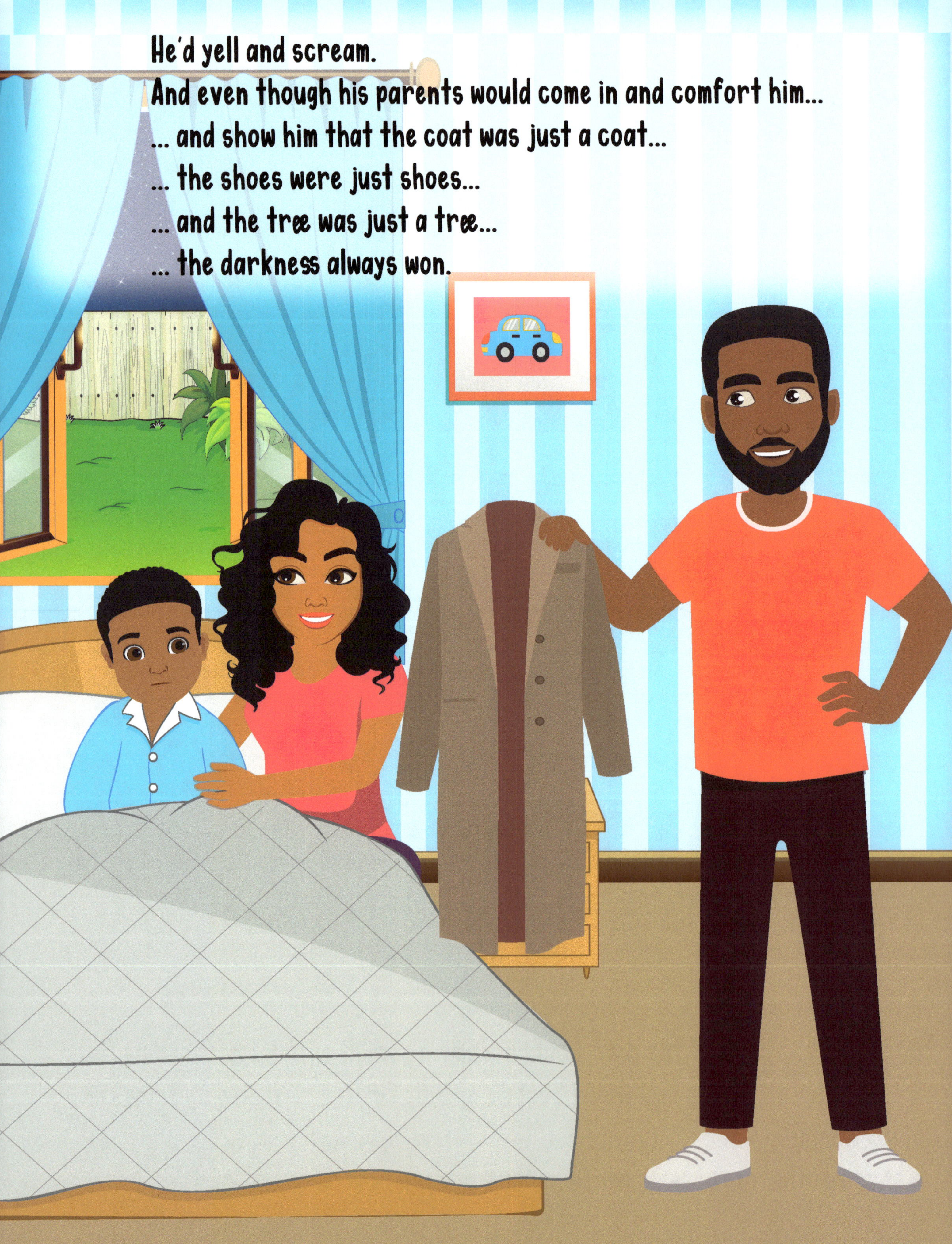

He'd yell and scream.
And even though his parents would come in and comfort him...
... and show him that the coat was just a coat...
... the shoes were just shoes...
... and the tree was just a tree...
... the darkness always won.

He never stayed in his bed the whole night.
Sometimes he would slip into his parents' bed.
Sometimes he would sleep with the dog by the fire.
He'd even been found sleeping in the bath before!
But whatever he and his parents' tried... nothing seemed to rid him of his fear.

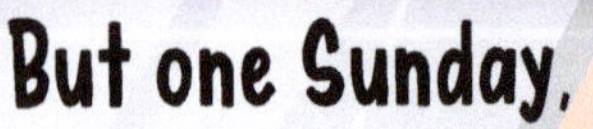

But one Sunday,
a Sunday that, to begin with, seemed no different from the rest,
something changed for Tré.
As usual, he spent the morning at the Children's Church at the end of his street.
As usual, he sat with all his friends on the floor.
As usual, he listened carefully to everything that their teacher, Mrs. Beacon,
had to say.

She read....

'Before the world began, there was the Word. The Word was with God, and the Word was God. He was with God in the beginning. All things were made through him. Nothing was made without him. In him there was life. That life was light for the people of the world. The Light shines in the darkness. And the darkness has not overpowered the Light.'

So, the Word,' explained Mrs. Beacon. 'Is what we also know as the Holy Spirit.'
'So, does that mean, it's the Holy Spirit who is a 'light for the people of the world'?' asked Tré.
'Well done, Tré,' said Mrs. Beacon. 'That's exactly right!'

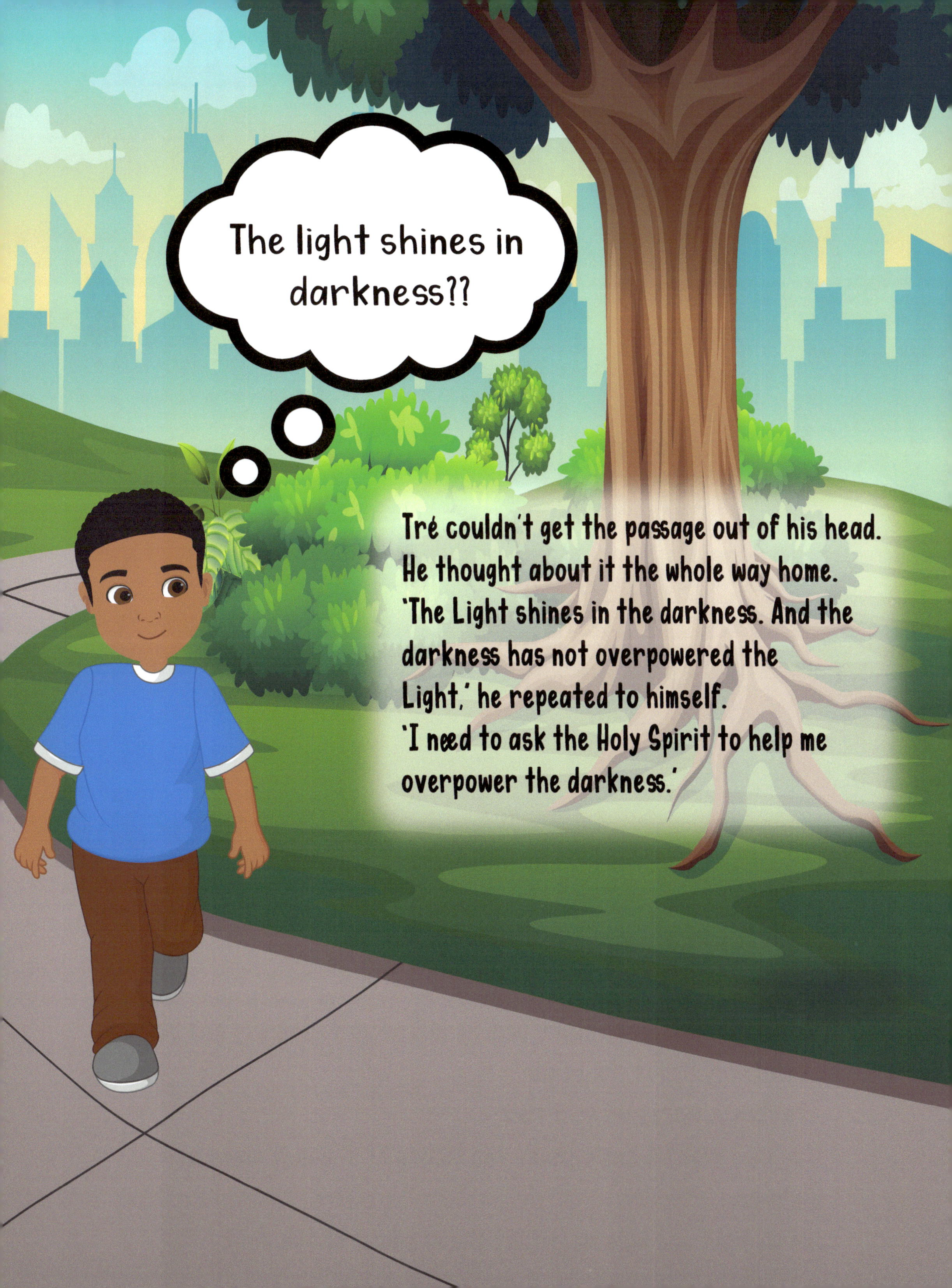

Tré couldn't get the passage out of his head. He thought about it the whole way home. 'The Light shines in the darkness. And the darkness has not overpowered the Light,' he repeated to himself.
'I need to ask the Holy Spirit to help me overpower the darkness.'

So that night, just before bed, he looked up to the sky and prayed.
'Dear Holy Spirit,' he began.
'Darkness makes me so afraid.
Try as I might, I can't shake the feeling of dread it gives me.
Help me.
Be my light and help me defeat the shadows of the dark.'

in the dead of night,
as usual,
Tré awoke.
And there they were... the scary shadows...
... the coat gorilla, the spindly fingers, the tree witch.
Fear began to fill him up, as always.
Until suddenly...

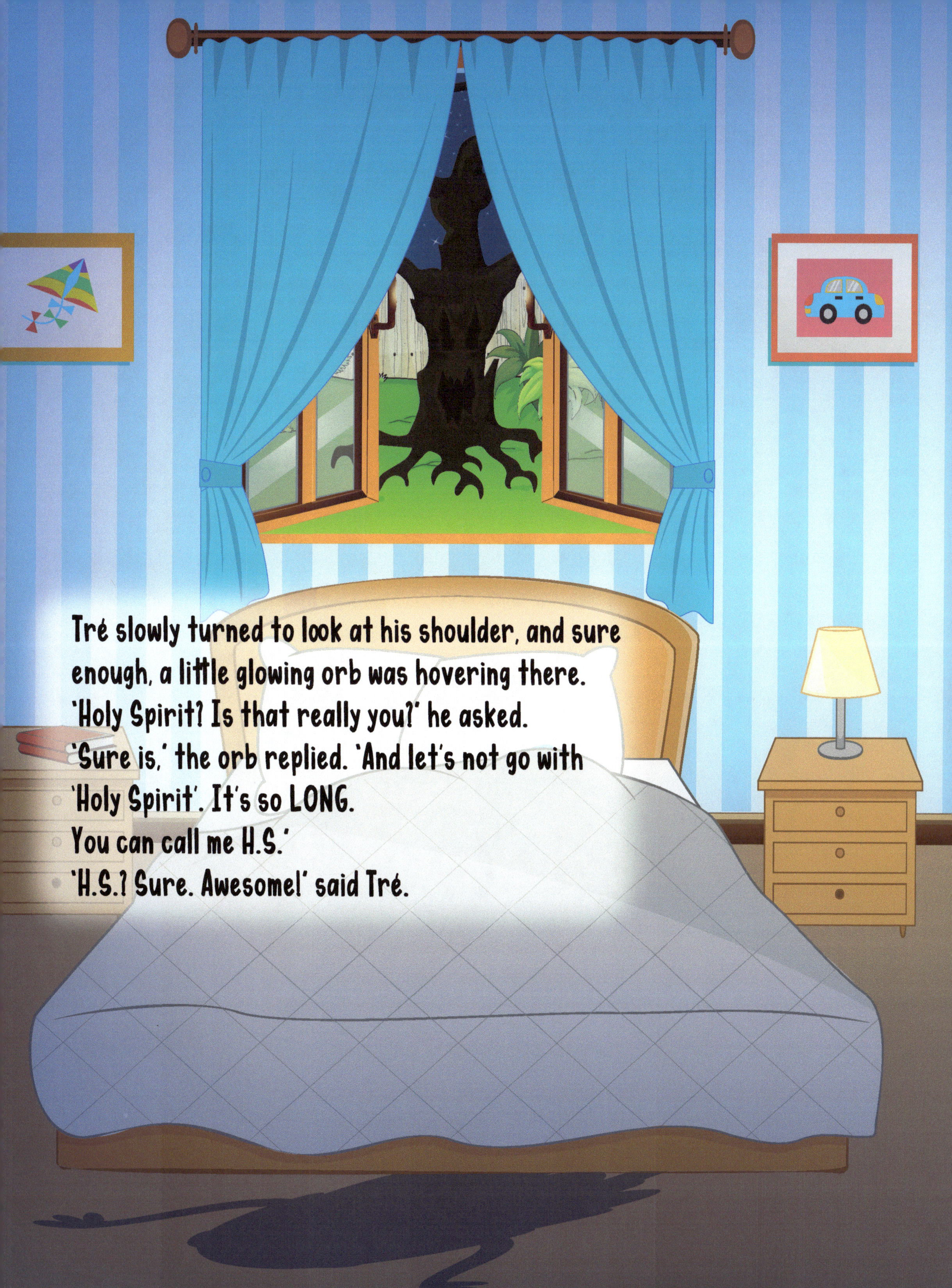

Tré slowly turned to look at his shoulder, and sure
enough, a little glowing orb was hovering there.
'Holy Spirit? Is that really you?' he asked.
'Sure is,' the orb replied. 'And let's not go with
'Holy Spirit'. It's so LONG.
You can call me H.S.'
'H.S.? Sure. Awesome!' said Tré.

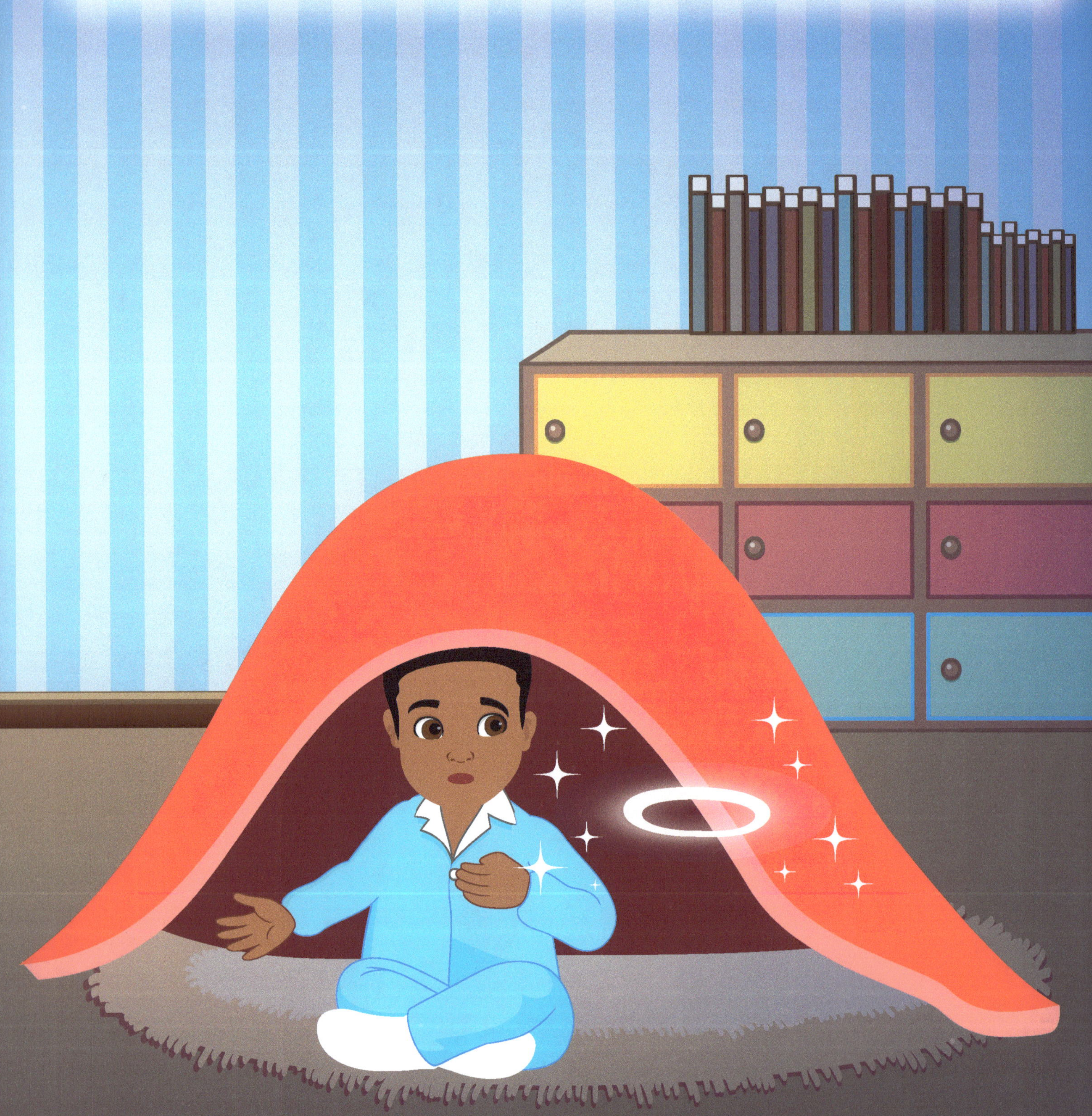
'Great,' said H.S. 'Now, you've got a darkness problem, right?'
'I sure do,' said Tré.
'OK, well I gotta few things to say about that!' said H.S.

'Number ONE!' he said.
'Darkness does not exist if you have a light within your heart.
Let the Father, Son, and the Holy Ghost (that's me) into your heart, and you'll never be without light again.'

'Number TWO!
Have you ever heard of a kid with gorillas, monsters, and witches in their room?'
'Ummm... no?' said Tré.
'That's right!' said H.S. 'No!
You know it's just the dark doing the Devil's work.
It's tricking you!'

'Number THREE.
You gotta know...
You are amazing.
You are strong.
You are bigger than the darkness.
You got this.
Whenever the darkness is creeping in and
playing tricks on you,
You gotta stand up to it and say,
loud and proud,
'SETTLE UP DARK!'.
You think you can do that?'
'I think so!' said Tré.

'Well go ahead,' said H.S. 'Give it a go.'
Tré turned back to face his bedroom.
The coat gorilla, the spindly fingers, and the tree witch seemed scarier
than ever. A lamp had also turned into an octopus, a chair into a giant
bug, and a hat into a skull

You got this,' whispered H.S.
'And I've got you.'
As the creatures loomed over him, Tré took a big breath.
He stood up, held out his hand, closed his eyes, and shouted
as loud as he could...
'SETTLE UP DARK!'

As the echo of his voice died down, he slowly opened his eyes.
The coat was now just a coat.
The tree... a tree, the shoes... some shoes, the lamp, chair, and hat... a lamp, chair, and hat.
Tré had done it.
And now, with the Holy Spirit on his shoulder, he felt like he could do anything.

If ever he was in a dark tunnel,
where the wind whistled like a ghost's breath,
and the vines creeping up the walls looked like snakes and worms,
Tré would hold out his hand,
yell, 'SETTLE UP DARK!',
and all would be well.
"SETTLE UP DARK!"

If ever he was on a gloomy street,
where the dripping rain sounded like
sharpening knives,
and the rumbling thunder sounded
like a beast clearing its throat,
Tré would hold out his hand,
yell, 'SETTLE UP DARK!',
and his heart would calm.

If ever he was in a murky forest,
where the birds sounded like dinosaurs,
and bushes looked like trolls,
Tré would hold out his hand,
yell, 'SETTLE UP DARK!',
and the darkness would have power
no more.

The Holy Spirit never left his side.
Knowing that he carried him within his heart
wherever he went, meant that he knew he
was never alone.
With Holy Spirit by his side, there was never any
need for fear again